More Fireflies

Poetry

Kendall Johnson

ARROYO SECO PRESS

Logo by Morgan G Robles
morganrobles.carbonmade.com

Arroyo Seco Press

www.arroyosecopress.org

Cover art: Kendall Johnson

ISBN 13: 978-1-7326911-6-2
ISBN 10: 1-7326911-6-9

This book is dedicated to my wife, muse, and patient listener, Susan Ilsley.

Poems

Note to the Reader

When 2020 rolled to a close I was grateful, scarcely imagining that the new year could get worse. Yet media spectacle bombards us every hour with new, more frightening atrocities and threat. We fight over what is right, real, or true. We find ourselves driving a rough road through dark night. In the face of the grinding uncertainty that is today, what can we look toward for the courage to continue? I penned FIREFLIES AGAINST DARKNESS to give a partial answer.

Many found that collection heartening. Now 2022 has arrived, and in many ways our situation is worse. I found myself discovering more stories for my own comfort, something I could do in response. Here they are.

I. Multiple Sources

1. New Year's Day, 2022
2. Biden and Putin exchange warnings over Ukraine
3. China harvests masses of data on Western Targets
4. Winter forest fire near Boulder burns 1,000 houses, 30,000 evacuated
5. 65 shots fired on busy Philadelphia street on New Year's Eve
6. 6,500 flights scrubbed nationally between Christmas and New Year, due to Covid-19
7. New data shows that forest fires release stored gamma radiation
8. Map application on cell phones misdirects hundreds into perilous snow storm
9. Despite 80,000 confirmed Covid-19 cases in New York, 15,000 revelers gathered in Times Square to watch the ball drop
10. Fish fall from sky during rainstorms in eastern Texas

this brief moment
ten thousand stars
open your eyes

II. Some Challenged Artists Stories

History shows many artists and writers struggling against not only the normal challenges of their art, but often daily personal and social instabilities as well. A few cases:

1. Poverty, possible Autism
2. Violence, murder
3. Psychosis, suicidal
4. Alcoholism, suicidal
5. Recluse, suicidal
6. Delusional, hospitalization
7. Addiction, bizarre behavior
8. Alcoholism
9. Depression
10. Paranoia

We know them by name as: Michelangelo, Caravaggio, van Gogh, Gauguin, Dickenson, Dadd, Dali, Pollock, Rothko, and Basquiat.

III. NBC Polling

Voters' Beliefs Revealed:
According to a recent NBC poll, sixty-four percent of
Americans have refused full vaccination, despite the
availability of free vaccine. Anti-vaxxers claim microchips in
the vaccine, alterations in DNA, that vaccine "sheds"
contaminating those in close vicinity, that vaccine causes
variants, and that vaccine has led to large numbers of deaths.
Reluctance continues despite the fact that all of these theories
have been debunked. A full fifteen percent of Americans
actually agree with the statement that the worlds of
government, media, and business are controlled by "Satan-
worshipping pedophiles" running a global child sex
trafficking operation." Fully one-third of American
Millennials believe that the earth is flat, and that scientific
evidence to the contrary is conspiracy. One of the Flat Earth
Society groups on Facebook has 227,031 followers.

looking upward
you watch stars and moons
form and disappear

IV. Keanu's Story

Sometimes it's easy to figure hardship is a recipe for lost dreams. But sometimes not so. Take actor Keanau Reeves:

- Three different stepfathers
- Dyslexic
- Serious accident ending his dream of a sports career
- Daughter died at birth
- Wife died in car accident
- Best friend dies of overdose
- Sister has leukemia

Keanu Reeves goes on to be a success. As an actor, of course, but more than that. This man is known for his compassion, generosity, and acts of kindness spending time and money listening to strangers, taking time to walk with them, listening to their stories.

V. British Oxford Dictionary

A few years ago, just in time, the British Oxford Dictionary made "<u>post-truth</u>" the word of the year. They point to some characteristics and strategies of "post-truth" discourse:

> Counter-narratives
> Gaslighting
> Shifting blame
> Discrediting critics
> Denial of facts
> Distrust of experts
> Privileging beliefs and opinion
> Denial of responsibility
> Tribal epistemologies
> Persuasion over evidence
> Emotion over reason
> Epistemic insouciance
> and Fake News.

space in limitless depth
surrounds tiny blues and greens
you fall closer

VI. Will's Story

Will and Elee were inseparable, one of those too-good-to-be-true couples whose marriage was a rewarding adventure. Preacher's kids, they found adventure in other cultures and other peoples, and not only studied and traveled extensively, but opened their homes to other "Couchsurfers," welcoming out-of-town travelers into their home. Many of these strangers became friends. When Elee was dying from a resurgent breast cancer, she asked only one thing of Will: that he continue traveling and opening their home to strangers. She believed that it would be through outreach to strangers that Will could find healing. After death, Will followed Elee's suggestion, traveling and living in far-off lands. He found his solace in the company of people who have now become close friends. He has even written of his experiences of healing in a book. The subtitle includes "How We Find Connection in a Disconnected World."

VII. Fox News

Not content with character assassination, a conservative newscaster called for physical action against a non-partisan health official in order to pander to the newscaster's right-wing viewership. In a tone reminiscent of Trump's encouragement of violent rioters on January 6, 2020, Fox News host Jesse Watters called for an ambush:

> "Now you go in for the kill shot . . . an ambush. Deadly. Because he doesn't see it coming,"

Fox News executives again declined to comment.

you watch the landmass
break into main pieces which
float into constant rotating shift

VIII. Dave's Story

My friend Dave, who suffered from brutal bouts of depression, was elated. "Read this book," he told me, handing me William Styron's *Darkness Visible*. "It's the first time I've ever heard anyone share their depression, and how it really feels inside. I didn't think anyone else goes through this." Dave's family was from Russia, where Stalin had killed some 40 million Jews, including some of Dave's own family.

Dave was more animated than I'd ever seen him. "My God," Dave exclaimed, his eyes bright. "His depression was worse than mine. And he is still here, still writing! And what he is writing is very good!"

IX. WUSA9, Washington D.C.

School Board Violence

Citing over twenty verified incidents of "death threats, disruptions, and violence," the National School Boards Association has requested investigation by the Federal Bureau of Investigation and the National Threat Assessment Center. Crucial to providing community representation in local school policy, school board meetings have become dangerous to attend due to threats and intimidation by extreme political groups. School board members and their families face personal threats and harassment by attendees angered by Covid-19 restrictions, mask requirements, conspiracy theories, and unfounded fear stoked by irresponsible and inflammatory political rhetoric.

where they slowly collide,
mountain ranges rise and fall
continents dance through time

X. Victor's Story

Dr. Victor Frankl was a successful psychiatrist in Vienna, specializing in the treatment of adolescent suicide. When the Nazis invaded Austria, he was first unable to practice, then thrown into the death camps where his father, mother, brother and wife were killed. It is there, in one of the darkest moments of human history, when all was lost, that he served his other inmates as medic, helping them fight to live, watching them die. During this time, he made a critical observation. Those prisoners who lived, he found, were those who had a reason to live. From this he deduced that the will to meaning is central to human well-being. He himself decided to live, in spite of his losing everything, so that he could share this insight with the world.

XI. YAHOO NEWS

Oxfam, the British confederation of 21 independent charitable organizations focusing on famine relief, issues an annual report. Their January 2022 report shows that the pandemic has made the wealthy wealthier, and the world's ten richest men have more than doubled their fortunes since March 2020. At the same time, lowered incomes of the world's poorest have contributed to the deaths of 21,000 each day.

disruption forms shapes
mountains from the plains
rivers melt rock into sea

XII. Deepa's Story

Deepa Biswas was born in Calcutta in 1941. Her free-thinking mother had been deprived of education when married off by her own brother. Every day Deepa walked among the starving poor, whom she vowed someday to help. Deepa studied under Mother Theresa at Loretto Convent, then qualified for a U.S. State Department grant, traveling to Wisconsin for graduate work. In 1968 she went to Memphis to march with Dr. Martin Luther King, and was there when he was killed. Later her work drew her to Santa Barbara, California with advanced degrees and her new husband. They were riding a motorcycle one day when hit by a drunk. Her husband died, and she was left in debilitating pain and walked with a limp. She ended up working as a hospital administrator in Santa Ynez, joining the local Rotary Club. At the club member's urging, she took the opportunity to create an educational fund for girls. Deepa Biswas Willingham opened her first school in Calcutta—the heart of the human trafficking center of the world—where she provides girls safety, education, and most importantly, belief in their own worth.

XIII. Reuters

The litany of woes has increased again. New evidence out of
Texas indicates that pandemic stress directly contributes to
the recent upsurge in school shootings. And why? The study
cites the skyrocketing rise in community violence, breakdowns
in family structures, rising mental health needs related to
financial difficulties. Disrupted schedules, routines, and lack
of oversight at home contribute. The hidden factor, the
report reveals, is the lack of teachers and specialists trained
to manage violence. Staff leaving schools cite stress, divisiveness
and parent hostility as causes for leaving the field.

closer now you see
algae to plant to animal
spreading over the earth

XIV. Zhang's Story

Born into a family of accomplished artists in the beginning of the twentieth century, Zhang Daqian studied with the masters of his time and became one of China's finest traditional painters. Known particularly for exquisite watercolor landscape and lotus florals, his mastery of a variety of meticulous brush techniques was unsurpassed. But over time his eyesight deteriorated, threatening the end of his storied career. Zhang Daquin responded by moving ahead, developing a unique landscape technique no one before him had attempted. His new paintings—suggestive, moody, infused with areas of richly splashed color— eventually commanded greater acclaim and higher prices than the older, tradition-based works. They are now part of the established canon of modern Chinese painting.

XV. Bloomberg

Johns Hopkins University reported today that the Covid-19 Omicron variant pushed the total case number in the U.S. over one million new cases in one day. Despite urgent recommendations from U.S. health officials to vaccinate, and despite the availability of free vaccine, only 61% of Americans are fully vaccinated.

separate bits
of living stuff all go home
to the sea.

XVI. Ludwig's Story

Drafted into the Kaiser's army at the beginning of World
War I, when he was visiting home in Austria between terms
at Cambridge, Ludwig served in the infantry during some of
the worst fighting: first in the north against the British, then
on the Russian front in winter, and finally in the Dolomites
to the south as a Lieutenant in an artillery unit where he was
overrun and taken prisoner. All this time he carried a
manuscript of notes in his backpack, which he completed—
some say—on stolen toilet paper in the frozen POW camp in
the Italian Alps. The book? Ludwig Wittgenstein's *Logico
Tractatus Philosophicus*, argued by notables as the most
important philosophic breakthrough of the 20th Century.

XVII. NBC News Hour

Scientists report that the key ice shelf in front of the
Thwaites Glacier in Western Antarctica is melting faster than
expected. The Thwaites Glacier is about the size of Florida.
When it breaks up—recent estimates now in less than five
years—coastlines around the world will be affected. David
Holland, newly appointed fellow to the American
Geophysical Union, reports that new currents of warm
water are melting the ice shelf that holds back the glacier.
When it gives way the glacier, the largest in the world, will
move quickly into the sea. Holland foresees the sea level
rising several feet. The global coastline will be reformed, and
the hundreds of millions of people living on those coastlines
will be inundated and be forced to migrate.

born into the world
this cosmic dance of light and dark
a brief moment

XVIII. Michael's Story

Michael's reconnaissance unit was operating behind the lines in Vietnam, a war without those reassuring lines. An accident separated him from his people. Somehow, he bound the bones of his broken leg together with sinew and torn, muddy cloth, cross braced with a dirty stick, and crawled three nights and days back to his unit. After years of flashbacks and learning new skills Michael found glass blowing. The transparency, pliability and brittleness of the medium felt right and drew him further, fragile metaphor for the pain he knew so well. Eventually he found himself embarked on a series of bone-like pieces joined at right angles, braced with soft material. The series continues, and Michael's work is shown nationwide, recognized and appreciated especially by veterans.

XIX. Business Today

The bad news today is Chernobyl. In 1986, Unit Four of the
Soviet nuclear power project in the Ukraine exploded, killing
50 people at the time and sending a radioactive cloud over
much of Europe. The blast equaled that of 10 Hiroshima-
sized atomic bombs. The radiation killed an estimated 6-
8,000 in subsequent years. Now, thirty-five years later,
scientists are reporting recently elevated neutron levels
emanating from the ruins of the reactor. Despite attempts to
bury the melted reactor under tons of cement ("The Shelter"),
rainwater has permeated the block and reactivated the
radiation process. Anatolii Doroshenko of the Institute for
Safety Problems of Nuclear Power Plants reports an
alarming uptick of radiation emissions from an inaccessible
underground room called 305/2. Another scientist can't rule
out the possibility of an "accident." A third scientist
describes the ruins "smoldering like embers in a barbecue
pit."

birth and death
this particular world
being and no

XX. Etty's Story

The world has seen countless times of great darkness. The early 1940s in Holland was one of those times, especially if you were Jewish. Etty Hillesum was 27 when the Nazis entered Amsterdam, and like others, Etty kept a diary. In it, through her suffering, she records her spiritual change of heart. Through her diary, we read of her study of central texts of Jewish mysticism, the poetry of Rilke, Meister Eckhart. "I shall not burden myself with my fears," she writes. This young woman, who served as a volunteer social worker in the Westerbork transit camp, who knew she was likely destined for the death camps to the east, practiced a mindfulness to live fully anyway. We witness how she came to see beyond the pain and brutality, to focus upon the beauty and wonder and mystery of the world beyond circumstance, a world that is always still there.

XXI. Time

Anxiety and depression are spreading in the wake of the fifth wave of pandemic, characterized by loneliness and exhaustion, as is the growing fear that Covid-19 may become unending. The decline in mental health has become one of the emerging widespread symptoms. A teacher in Russia states "you watch apocalypse films and realize their writers were prophets." Normalcy remains elusive.

how close
we each live to the edge of night
each hour of our days

XXII. The Army's Story

It's tempting to listen to news reports that say that our lives are "nasty, brutish, and short," that we are violent killers in our human state of nature. Not so, says none other than the U.S. Army. When it sent Colonel Samuel Marshall onto the Civil War battlefield to study killing efficiency, Samuel found that most soldiers hadn't fired their weapons. Repeated studies over the last hundred and fifty years show that, even in desperate, do-or-die combat only twenty percent pull the trigger. Murder, Col. Marshall and the scientists who followed him found time after time, is simply not in our nature. The Army now uses special trainers and techniques to overcome "failure to fire." Turns out it takes special conditioning to train soldiers to kill.

XXIII. New York Times

Flying in the face of evidence, right wing commentators persist in spreading three key myths about the pandemic. Under the flag of freedom of speech, they claim that the Covid-19 is no big deal, that vaccinations are not effective, and that vaccinations are a matter of freedom of choice. On this logic, it would seem that syphilis should go untreated because some cases might be untreatable, that it isn't important because not everyone has it, and that both treatment and unprotected sex should be matters of personal whimsy for those who carry it.

comets, stellar bursts
whole galaxies colliding
you find your way back

XXIV. Alexa's Story

The painted wall of the room looks flat, then part of it moves and walks away. Or, down a normal street, a flat painted cut-out person in jagged black and white walks by looking very much alive. Body paint head to foot, you realize. Artist Alexa Meade playfully surprises and beguiles us into questioning just what is real, and just where we stand within that real. As the painted model dances out of her context again, your view of her world—and your place in yours— shifts all over once more.

XXV. NY Times

A synthesis of rigorous studies from the US and abroad
conducted by the Council on Criminal Justice cites a nearly
ten percent increase in domestic violence since pandemic
stay-at-home orders. The average rates of countries studied
were 7.9%, but the US rate was 8.1%.

Planets break orbits
gravitational pull throwing
neighbors in chaos

XXVI. Henri's Story

Accomplished artists evolve their craft over decades of sequenced development. It is soul work, learning just what approaches convey an idea to others when those ideas are themselves in constant evolution. Henri Matisse was one of those emergent geniuses—his experiments and collaborations in concepts, media, methods, and priorities became fuller and more articulated through the course of his pivotal career. This all nearly came to an end when two disabilities struck in later life. He developed cataracts which prevented him working close, in detail. Then radical surgery confined him to sitting in a wheelchair. Yet Henri, unable to grasp brushes, unable to stand far enough away from a canvas to focus, somehow found his way forward in the midst of this darkness. Rather than give up in the face of adversity, using assistants to reach, carry, place, and manipulate, Matisse spent the last fifteen years of his life developing the important artistic to innovations for which he is now recognized and famous.

XXVII. NY Times

Steep surge in auto traffic deaths attributed to Covid-19 mental health. Mortality rates on highways have been on a steady decline since the 1940s due to auto safety, enforcement, and lower speed limits. That all changed by the summer of 2020, and the rate is still on the increase. Experts believe that the increase is due to erratic behavior and aggressive driving related to stress due to uncertainties and changes imposed by Covid-19 restrictions, despite fewer vehicles on the road. The stress has resulted in higher anxiety, fraying social behavior, and the purchase of heavier, more protective and hence more dangerous, vehicles.

as you enter a sky
milky way lights your way
back to beginnings

XXVIII. Agatha's Story

Few writers begin famous. Shortly following the death of her beloved mother, her husband of fourteen years suddenly divorced her for another woman. Devastated, the double loss threw Agatha into a bleak depression and breakdown. She resisted suicide only because of her young daughter. Four years later Agatha journeyed on the legendary Orient Express to Istanbul, there meeting and marrying an archeologist. With her subsequent visits to sites in North Africa and the middle east, she wove together many of her subsequent iconic mysteries including *Death on the Nile* and *Murder on the Orient Express*. Best-selling fiction writer of all time, Agatha Christie, now Dame of the British Empire for her contributions to literature.

XXIX. PBS

Myths can kill. Info-tainment commentators spread myths and withhold important facts. They ignore:

1. The fact of nearly 1,000,000 deaths in the US so far.
2. The fact that relatively few fully vaccinated people die in hospitals from Covid-19, and
3. The fact that those who are refusing vaccination are the primary ones responsible for the spread of Covid-19 to others.

Measurable, proven facts. Instead, they choose to perpetuate harmful myths that in turn perpetuate the disease. They conveniently ignore another fact: that one person's right to swing their arm ends where another's nose begins.

you pull upward
through convection columns and winds
you fly toward the moon

XXX. Rotterdam's Story

Covid-19 shutdowns came as body-blows to businesses around the world. Live performances in the arts were especially hard hit. Not all folded, however. Adjusting to the emerging series of new realities, many organizations responded creatively and toward a greater good. Example: on March 20, 2020, the Rotterdam Philharmonic Orchestra pulled off a great experiment. Contending with problems of synchronization, platform integration, and sound quality, Rotterdam produced a performance with 19 of its musicians playing from each of their socially isolated homes. Beethoven's Ninth Symphony, his *Ode to Joy*, captured on YouTube, viewed some three million times.

XXXI. Scientific American

In a first-person account, a critical care nurse reports on the rage and exhaustion she and her colleagues deal with daily as they confront the hate, irrationality, and blame half the public displaces on them. She watches those with whom she works develop trauma symptoms, dark circles under their eyes, and the "brilliant lights of their souls dimming," in the face of the cynical disinformation.

for this time, here
you are born the great bird
a messenger

XXXII. Marie-Madeleine's Story

As Nazis marched into Paris in 1940, many French citizens
accepted allegiance to Marshal Pétain's collaborationist
"Vichy" government. A valiant few did not. When the leader
of the French Resistance was arrested, he selected Marie-
Madeleine Fourchade to lead in his place. She chose her code
name—Hedgehog—and set out to recruit her team of
operatives, pilots, couriers. Their mission: avoid and
sabotage Nazi occupiers and their Vichy collaborators in
conjunction with British intelligence by gathering
information, attacking telephone and rail facilities, and even
hiding and returning downed Allied aircrews. Marie-
Madeleine was captured four times and escaped four times.
While many of her fellow citizens kept their heads down,
Mme. Fourchade risked everything to stand up to the
darkness.

Acknowledgements

Many thanks to John Brantingham and his several writing circles, who gave constructive feedback on several of these pieces, for Kate Flannery who discussed the several iterations each took, to Elizabeth Buff Wright for manuscript editing, and for the several writers who provided valuable commentary. Most of all for the various souls who lived out inspiration for the stories, the fireflies whose live provide the rest of us such hope. In particular, respect and appreciation for writer and publisher Thomas R. Thomas whose work provides voice to the world for the writers within his pages.

Biography

Kendall Johnson, recently retired from his work in teaching, psychotherapy, and consulting on scene with emergency and disaster agencies, now paints and writes in Southern California. He is the author of *Dear Vincent: An Artist and Psychologist Writes Back to Van Gogh*; the nonfiction *Chaos & Ash*; *Black Box Poetics: Short Memoirs of Chaos*

In life and in print, Kendall Johnson IS this title and believes in its tiny promises. His words are both heart-breaking and heart-mending—but most of all they encourage hope. No matter how dark the circumstance, man-caused or natural, his beautifully-wrought words are spare beacons, truly *Fireflies Against Darkness*.

My Mum always told me to make friends with the folks in my lifeboat. I shall always wish Kendall Johnson were among them! With his initial *Fireflies Against Darkness*, he reminded us in his beautiful, poetic way that hope may not conquer all, but it is the most powerful armor we have against adversity. In this equally affecting sequel, he shows us the power, unwitting—perhaps unwilling—and everyday heroes possess in very small boats with hope at the helm.
—Tracey Meloni, Writer, *Nursing Education*

When times are tough, like they have been lately, we sometimes need help to get through. Kendall Johnson gives us that in Fireflies Against Darkness. Short hard news pieces are followed by tiny verses that, like fireflies, light the path connecting us to quietly courageous people who, using art or music or nature, bring us hope. Bring us out of the darkness. I love this book!

I was so heartened by reading *More Fireflies*, a continuation of the first collection. We really do need more of these uplifting stories and poem snippets to help counteract the tough news we've been hearing everyday.
—Louella Lester, author of *Glass Bricks*

This remarkable, highly original chapbook juxtaposes bulletins from the COVID-pandemic, out of control wildfires, natural disasters, mass shootings, and climate change chaos with glimpses of the famous (and not so famous) denizens of the art world and their struggles, including Chuck Close, Georgia and Ida O'Keeffe, and Vincent Van Gogh. I could not stop reading this mesmerizing collection. I didn't want it to end. Kendall Johnson has written something important, holding up a mirror to our tarnished reality.

What a joy to read *More Fireflies*, Kendall Johnson's sequel to his remarkable chapbook *Fireflies Against Darkness*. As someone who savored the first offering, I eagerly read this new volume. I was not disappointed.
—Alexis Rhone Fancher, author of *EROTIC: New & Selected, poetry*, editor, Cultural Daily

When times are tough, like they have been lately, we sometimes need help to get through. Kendall Johnson gives us that in Fireflies Against Darkness. Short hard news pieces are followed by tiny verses that, like fireflies, light the path connecting us to quietly courageous people who, using art or music or nature, bring us hope. Bring us out of the darkness. I love this book!

Once again, in his second Fireflies book *More Fireflies*, Kendall Johnson has given us flashes of magic and hope in a bleak and disturbing world—magic and hope that are enduring and soul-deep. Johnson has known darkness of the heart, both in his personal life as a Vietnam veteran and later as a psychologist specializing in the treatment of severe trauma. And he doesn't hesitate to share some of that darkness in this new volume. But, as he did before, he is persistently driven to move us beyond that point where we lose trust in humanity. His "fireflies," small tales and glimpses of individual perseverance, generosity, and strength, are stunning reflections on the power of human goodness and the creative mind. If you are ever close to despair, you will want to hang on to Johnson's *More Fireflies* like the lifeline it is.

—Kate Flannery, Writer of *Ekphrasis for the Sasse Museum of Art, poetry,* and *memoir*

Kendall Johnson's *Fireflies against Darkness* is in the end a bright spot in a world that could seem endlessly painful. The author has seen more evil than any one person should have to see from his tour of Vietnam where young men were asked to savage a country and murder strangers, to New York City during the days of 9/11. Between and after that time, he has made a career of confronting evil through his practice as a trauma psychotherapist. What is extraordinary about him is that rather than being dragged down into that evil, he has fought to see the spots of light in an otherwise chaotic universe and to make them his practice. He has maintained his essential self, and this book is a guide for us to do the same.

With this second in the Fireflies series, Kendall Johnson has changed the way I see life and what is possible. There is pain, but there are always fireflies in the darkness. We are not alone, and the light has not yet been extinguished.

—John Brantingham, *Inaugural Poet Laureate, Sequoia Kings Canyon National Park*

48405392R50030